THE LOST FILMS FANZINE PRESENTS MOVIE MILESTONES #1 AUGUST 2020

EDITOR AND PUBLISHER: JOHN LEMAY/BICEP BOOKS
SPECIAL CONSULTANT: KYLE BYRD
SPECIAL THANKS THIS ISSUE TO MIKE BOGUE AND DON GLUT

EDITORIAL

Welcome to the debut issue of *Movie Milestones*, a subsidiary/spin-off of *The Lost Films Fanzine*. As the name "Movie Milestones" suggests, this magazine celebrates anniversaries, in this case the 80th anniversary of *One Million B.C.* (1940).

But wait, you say, that's all well and good, but isn't this a *Lost Films Fanzine* magazine? Yes, it is, and though the film in this issue is by no means lost, like all projects, it wasn't completed and released as originally envisioned. As we all know, *One Million B.C.* has been maligned for years due to using live lizards in place of stop motion dinosaurs. But, did you know that one of the film's producers wanted to go the stopmotion route, but was shot down by Hal Roach, the head honcho and eventual director?

B.C.'s better known remake, *One Million Years B.C.* (1966), also went through several tantalizing revisions. For certain, the original ending (wherein a brontosaurs attacks the Rock Tribe) was partially shot and then excised. Supposedly, narration was done that covered the film's full runtime, not just the opening! Seemingly small alterations like these could have made the movies into completely different films. Dare I say lost films...

To be very clear, this is not a magazine about the making of these films, so much as it's about the development of the films. Or, the roads not taken, if you prefer. Whereas many magazines and books have focused on what these films were, we're going to focus on what they could have been via original ideas, unfilmed and/or deleted scenes, and unproduced sequels.

And, finally, the most important reason I created this little magazine is because I love the movies within it. If you're reading this right now, chances are you do too. It's essentially my love letter to the B.C. films. So, with no more ado, I hope you appreciate this tribute to the more obscure aspects of these classic caveman films...

BEFORE ONE MILLION B.C.

Though everyone reading this magazine probably already knows that 1940's *One Million B.C.* is 1966's *One Million Years B.C.*'s great-granddaddy, *One Million B.C.* had its own grandparents and predecessors to thank for the caveman genre.

In fact, the very first dinosaur film ever shot focused on cavemen and dinosaurs. *Prehistoric Peeps* (1905) was based on a comic written and drawn by Edward Tennyson Reed starting in the 1890s. Supposedly the dinosaurs in the film were brought to life by men in costumes. I say supposedly because *Prehistoric Peeps* is a lost film.

In 1912, D.W. Griffith produced *Man's Genesis*, another caveman tale (sans dinosaurs). It begins in the modern day with a grandfather regaling his grandchildren with tales of the prehistoric age as they climb up a hill. It seemed to set the template for several similar films to follow, as it focused on a weak caveman trying to woo a cavewoman away from a strong alpha male. The story ends with the hero, Weakhands, developing the first club, to beat the villain, Bruteforce. In 1914, Griffith was at it again with *Brute Force*, a live-action comedy short that begins in the modern-day. A man named Harry is upset that his girlfriend, Priscilla, has left a party with another man. "Oh, for the good old days of brute force and marriage by capture!" Harry's title card reads.

Harry then has a flashback to the "good ol' days" of prehistoric times. In the scene, a caveman and his mate survive various perils, including something resembling a winged dragon more so than a dinosaur. Also popping up is a Ceratosaurus, animated via stop-motion. As such, this was the first stop-motion dinosaur ever created

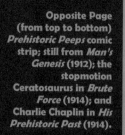

Opposite Page (from top to bottom) *Prehistoric Peeps* comic strip; still from *Man's Genesis* (1912); the stopmotion Ceratosaurus in *Brute Force* (1914); and Charlie Chaplin in *His Prehistoric Past* (1914).

This Page: Posters for *One Million B.C.* (1940) and the Super 8mm version.

Greatest THRILLS ON EARTH

The World at the Dawn of Time... Savage Cave Men and Weird Monsters that Stun the Senses... The Heroic Struggle of a Boy and Girl for Life and Primitive Love... SIGHTS ...WONDERS...THRILLS ...Never Before Beheld by Man!

So Amazing You won't believe your eyes!

Hal Roach presents

ONE MILLION B.C.

with

Victor MATURE · Carole LANDIS
Lon CHANEY, Jr.

Directed by HAL ROACH and HAL ROACH, Jr.
Released thru United Artists

See Real Pre-historic Beasts of Bygone Ages... Re-created and Filmed by a new secret process!

BATTLE of the GIANTS

CASTLE FILMS
FOR ALL HOME MOVIE PROJECTORS

YOU WON'T BELIEVE YOUR EYES!

Hal Roach presents

ONE MILLION B.C.

**Still from 1923's _The Three Ages_ (main)
and 1915's _The Missing Link_ (inset)**

Charlie Chaplin produced a similar prehistoric comedy that year too in _His Prehistoric Past_. Apparently 1914 was a big year for caveman movies, for it also saw the release of the short _The Primitive Man_!

Next came _The Dinosaur and the Missing Link: A Prehistoric Tragedy_, a short film animated by Willis O'Brien in 1915. The movie was released later, in 1917, by Thomas Edison's film company Conquest Pictures. The comical story followed the efforts of a caveman trying to impress a cavewoman, with his attempts being thwarted by an ape, the missing link. That same year saw the release of two more O'Brien spoofs. _R.F.D. 10,000 B.C._ focused yet again on rivalry between cavemen competing for a woman. In this case, one was a prehistoric mailman who rode a dinosaur on his route! _Prehistoric Poultry_ showcased a prehistoric chicken monster of a sort.

1923 saw the release of _The Three Ages_, a comedy starring Buster Keaton and Wallace Beery. As the title suggests, it takes place in three different periods, one of which is the prehistoric past. In the film, Keaton's caveman competes with the more beefy character played by Beery for the love of a cavewoman.

To the best of my knowledge, Hal Roach's 1940 production of _One Million B.C._, was the first feature-length caveman movie. Unlike its then-recent predecessors, 1925's _The Lost World_ and 1933's _King Kong_, it eschewed stop-motion effects in favor of men in suits and real animals disguised as dinosaurs.

Director: Hal Roach *Script*: George Baker, Mickell Novak, Joseph Frickert & D.W. Griffith (uncredited) *SPFX Director*: Hal Roach Jr. *Music*: Werner R. Heymann *Cast*: Victor Mature (Tumak) Carole Landis (Loana) Lon Chaney Jr. (Akhoba) Conrad Nagel (professor/narrator) *Release Date*: April 5, 1940 *Runtime*: 80 Minutes *Alternate Titles:* MAN AND HIS MATE, THE CAVE DWELLERS, TUMAK, CAVE MAN

Plot: Tumak, an outcast from the Rock Tribe, is found near death by the lovely Loana, of the peaceful Shell Tribe. The Stone Age lovers trek across an unforgiving prehistoric landscape and, in the end, a cataclysm causes their two tribes to band together into one.

Previous page: Victor Mature and Carole Landis (main) Spanish release poster (inset). Above: Colorized lobby card.

MAKING ONE MILLION B.C.

Today, *One Million B.C.* has a somewhat dubious reputation due to the fact that not only did it use real reptiles in place of special effect dinosaurs, but said reptiles were subjected to cruel treatment during filming (namely a forced battle to the death between two starved lizards). Furthermore, the reptile footage was recycled ad nauseam in dozens of other dinosaur pictures over the years. Despite these dubious distinctions, *B.C.* is still the true grandfather of the dinosaur-caveman genre. It also could have turned out very different...

To help prep his prehistoric epic, Hal Roach (primarily a producer of comedy shorts including the Laurel and Hardy series) courted none other than D.W. Griffith, who produced many of the previously discussed caveman movies.

Initially, the project was called *Life Begins* and Roach supposedly wanted Griffith to direct the film. It's unknown just how true this is, and more reliable sources state that Roach just wanted Griffith's name attached to the project as a producer. Rumors of Griffith as a potential director may have stemmed from the fact that Griffith helped to cast the actors, and also did their screen tests and costume fittings.

"Griffith did all the tests," recalled Victor Mature in a 1966 story in the *Los Angeles Times*. "He tested for six months. I don't know what he was looking for. They'd have been better off letting the old man direct the picture. One day he just wasn't around any more." Mature was insinuating that perhaps the film would have turned out better with Griffith at the helm.

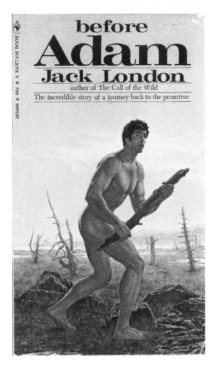

One of the influences behind *B.C.* was Jack London's 1907 novel, *Before Adam*. It featured a modern-day man who dreamt of being a caveman. Notably, it had tribes at varying levels of development, much like *B.C.* In the case of *Before Adam*, it featured the Cave People, the Tree People, and the Fire People. As to why Roach didn't simply adapt the novel, he couldn't. RKO's David O. Selznick had bought the rights years earlier with Lon Chaney Sr. in mind to star!

As with all completed films, there's a lost, un-shot version of *B.C.* that we'll never see. You see, Griffith left the production over disagreements with Roach. Griffith apparently wanted to give the cavemen greater characterization.

"Mr. Roach did not feel that it was necessary to give the characters as much individuality as I thought was needed, and so I did not wish to appear responsible for the picture

by having my name on it," Griffith told the *New York Times* on April 21, 1940.

What exactly would Griffith's true vision have looked like? That's tough to say, but supposedly he wrote the script based upon a French novel. However, this alleged novel by the conspicuously named "Eugene Roche" was probably just a publicity ploy made up by Roach. Eugene Roche, it is thought, was Roach's pen name for the *B.C.* story.

According to various sources, Griffith wrote several story treatments and at least one screenplay, said to run 76 pages. After reviewing these treatments, Roach handed off one of Griffith's outlines to the main scripter, George Baker, in mid-August of 1939. At the same time, for reasons unknown, Roach also had Griffith work on his own script! Griffith's 76 page script was described by Stuart Galbraith IV (who read it) as being a "sketchy affair." In his article, "Long

Top: The T-Rex suit (and one of the film's two non-lizard dinos) seen here was based upon a painting by Charles Knight and created by Fred Knoth. This suit was a quickly assembled prototype. Knoth had no intention of it being the final version, but once Roach saw it he loved it, so it was used. Insets: Two test frames of the dino-lizards. Middle: Publicity Float for the film. Bottom: Deleted Scene? Nope, just a publicity still of Landis atop the mammoth.

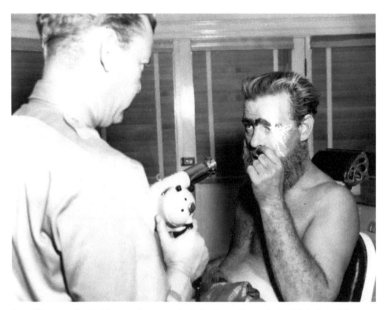

Lon Chaney Jr. in the make-up chair to transform into Akhoba. Chaney designed his own makeup for Akhoba, but couldn't use it due to Cosmetician's Union rules!

Ago Before Jurassic Park" in *Filmfax* #48, Galbraith wrote that the screenplay was "more akin to [Griffith's] manner of screenplay writing 20 years earlier—completely out of touch with the realities of modern film production..." [p.34]

In the absence of dialogue spoken by the main cave-characters, Griffith had scripted narration to help the audience follow the plot. Griffith also wanted the dinosaurs to be created via stopmotion, as had been done on *The Lost World* and *King Kong*. Roach did not. In fact, that "no animation" was used in *B.C.* was touted proudly by Roach in advertising as though it were an asset rather than a detriment!

Back to scripting, by contrast to Griffith's 76 page script, Baker turned in a 373-page screenplay, which he would later expand upon with Mickell Novak to 500 pages by October.

The initial script also had some differences. Notably, Roach was concerned with how to introduce the picture, especially since he had done away with Griffith's scripted narration. Therefore, it was decided to bookend the film with segments set in modern times with dialogue.

In the finished film, a group of hikers takes shelter in a cave. Inside they find a professor studying some ancient cave paintings. Notably, Victor Mature and Carole Landis appear as some of the hikers. The professor uses these two as examples as he interprets the cave drawings that tell the saga of Tumak and Loana.

Originally, as scripted, the film was to have Mature and Landis playing young archeologist students who show up late to a cave-side dig.

The film began shooting on November 6, 1939, under the title of *1,000,000 B.C.* Location shooting

Above: Colorized Lobby Card. Left: Victor Mature as Tumak. Roach's original choice for Tumak was Richard Denning, who would go on to star in another dinosaur picture, *Unknown Island* (1948).

though it's unknown just what these cut scenes entailed.

The film was a success at the box office, and if one were to exclude the roll-over receipts from *Gone With the Wind* into 1940, *One Million B.C.* was the highest grossing film that year. However, the critical reaction was mixed. B. R. Crisler of *The New York Times* called it "a masterpiece of imaginative fiction" while *Variety* described it as "corny." The film went on to be nominated for two Oscars, including Best Special Effects and Best Score.

As for Griffith, he had left the production before it had even begun shooting. Roach still wanted to put Griffith's name on the film (possibly as "Associate Producer") but Griffith asked not to be credited, as he was not impressed with the film.

was done 35 miles Northeast of Las Vegas, Nevada, and wrapped within a little over a week. The rest was shot in studio until the day after Christmas.

The film, now retitled *One Million B.C.*, ran before a test audience on Valentine's Day in 1940. Griffith cut several minute's worth of footage based upon the audience's reaction,

LIFE WAS LIKE THAT IN ONE MILLION B.C.!

Men Were Men—and Beasts Were Beasts— in Prehistoric Days when Giant Monsters Roamed the Earth

having developed a civilization based on kindliness and understanding, the other hand, is completely dominated by a fierce and terrible spirit and his body strikes fear. A common danger — attack by a dinosaur — do they for an instant forget their enmity and remember understanding.

"One Million B.C." was filmed from a story by screen writers Mickell Novak, George Baker and Joseph Frickert, and affects, incorporated in the picture, it was photographed on 365 miles from Los Angeles. Fire Valley is a fiery gash in the formation of sandstone which the elements have eroded into grotesque caves, chasms.

sue of those that lived in the Pleistocene, — Mesasaurus and the Plesiosaur. The close of the Cretaceous Period — the twilight of the dinosaur — marked a revolutionary era in the history of the earth, says Martin. Mother Nature went into far less destructive and remodeling on a grand scale. It was the biggest New Deal of all time.

Widespread adjustments in the earth's surface occurred. The Rocky Mountains, for instance, rose from the shifting in the shade of the giant reptiles, dried mendous volcanic action began and continued unabated into the Pleistocene period.

Martin, or Miocene, period the land that drained the marshes recaused fundamental changes that the weaker portions of the earth's folding. There was a resultant connection where faults accumulated miles long popped open when the Cretaceous soil. The fire for such a volume of jelly! Lava poured from many of these rifts and from the lowlands of Java and Sumatra.

our imaginations picture the plight of the dinosaurs when Volcanoes belched fire, was the story of Mount Pelee, on the island of Martinique. It overwhelmed the city of St. Pierre, killing every inhabitant but one, a negro prisoner who

following the explosion.

The explosion compares with the eruptions about as a pop gun compares with a sixteen inch cannon. The products of the eruption were carbon monoxide, sulphur dioxide.

Left, the skeleton of a prehistoric triceratops dug from the earth by paleontologists.

Right, a restoration of the same animal as he looked one million or more years ago.

twelve square miles and reached had been confined to a dungeon. 2800 feet into the heavens. It A rush of gas and dust, heavy and in fact, a hole nine hundred incandescent, burst into the hundred feet high, a vent for all dred feet much above the surface that much hot breathed. It passed swiftly and

sulphur trioxide, hydrogen, nitrogen, hydrogen sulphide, methane, carbonic acid gas, and hydrochloric acid. One authority very tentatively, almost innocently, says: "These gasses, thrown out from time to time, and noted loved near a smelter and still readily agrees with the good professor. And all the smellers in the world together could not generate enough gas for one good puff in even a small volcano.

"About one hundred five hundred volcanos active during historic time (ten thousand years) had hurled forth. Think of having, not five hundred, but five thousand very large and very active volcanos, belching away at the same time, and you get some idea of things near the close of the Cretaceous age.

"Mammals, underprivileged for millions of years, had an enormous existence, hiding in burrows by day, and venturing forth of years spent in hiding. Times, unless unusually potent, believed reptiles adept. The mammal was not allergic to dust, having built underground passages, in hollow trees and in caves, keeping places, would have overwhelmed an animal accustomed to breathing in his burrow and was saved from storms like the prisoner in his dungeon on Martinique.

"Some restorers of the small reptiles, restorers of those we know,

WHY did the dinosaurs die? Whence those huge, fear-ful-looking reptiles, and why that took their place on this earth?

What happened one million-odd years ago that the beasts which had flourished so long should disappear, abruptly and completely? At the time of their downfall, the dinosaurs ruled supreme, both in size and numbers. They ruled the land, sea and air. Then —

Science's answer is drastic and dramatic — that was the death of the dinosaurs.

Speaking geologically, biologically speaking, the demise of a type of animal is a drawn out, gradual process. There are times in which man has noted the extinction of species through ruthless slaughter or by taking over the land and food supply. The rocks record these fade-outs. The strata of one period is rich in some animal remains; the next layer contains fewer remains, and the fossils become scarcer and scarcer until they disappear entirely.

It was not like that with the dinosaurs. They vanished from the close of the Cretaceous period, about 60 million years back. Their huge bones have been found in

variety and numbers in rock formations of that age. But at that place —

Several theories have been advanced to explain the phenomenon of their death. This suddenness, because of a change in climatic conditions. They either froze or cooked to death. For the dinosaur was cold-blooded. Their body temperature rose and fell with the temperature of their surroundings. Unlike mammals, including man, they could not stand extremes of cold and heat. Thus, desolate exposed to the sizzling desert sun dies quickly. A reptile or a mammal with a warm-blooded or than its customary habitat becomes a helpless creature, its life processes retarded, so that it is easy prey to any enemy that happens along.

It might have been with the dinosaurs, the scientists with the slight change either way in the temperature of the earth could have killed them.

Primitive men fight off a huge reptilian beast which invades their cave in "One Million B. C.," Hollywood's imaginative recreation of mankind's dawn period.

thousands of craters forming 'the circle of fire that girdled the Pacific. Imagination breaks down when one tries to form a mental picture of the mighty force that suddenly became demonstrative after millions of years of quiescence, as 'how followed the earth formations, thousands of feet thick and burning, Usually brilliant sunsets were noted as a result of this dust for three years be remembered that such demon-

"Volcanos have played a very great part in present day geography. At the present day, even but a limestone cap formed at the top of a great volcano. Hundreds of such masses have similarly been forming coral reefs formed on volcanic extrusions.

"Something occurred at ten A.M. August 27, 1883, that helps

and killed from thirty to forty thousand people. The sound was heard for three thousand miles before this final rush of hot gas, the volcano had given warning by emitting puffs gases that had killed horses on the streets of St. Pierre and caused considerable

"This seems terrific, but it must

Left, death struggle between an iguanodon and an allosaurus as visualized by artist Heinrich Harder. Right, balm for the wounds of a prehistoric huntsman. Victor Mature and Carole Landis portray a youth and maiden in "One Million B. C."

Some of Martin's wood statues of extinct beasts are in the Smithsonian Institute at Washington, D.C. He has, through incessant research and study, learned that whose remains have been found in the famous La Brea Tar Pits in the neighborhood of Los Angeles. He recently finished and turned over to the museum the motion picture "One Million B.C." This is a film dealing with the monsters of prehistoric times. Hal Roach, the producer, who produced and directed "One Million B.C.," called a film spectacle of pre-historic times, "One Million B.C." deals with the exploits of the Rock Tribe in fighting volcanoes and earthquakes. It also shows how these caveman lived in constant danger of attack from dinosaurs, mammoths, huge reptiles, musk oxen and many other gigantic beasts of a remote era.

The picture also makes the interesting point that even in caveman days there were vast differences in the various tribes. People are shown to be more progressive than the Rock Tribe,

peaks and pillars. This part of the country ... is the kind of wild, prehistoric setting required for the picture.

There prehistoric creatures were also photographed in this valley. In addition to the assortment of life-sized dinosaurs which come to life on the screen, there are also giant reptiles of past eras are also on parade. How they were assembled remains a secret with Producer Roach and his staff. Even the stars, the film — Lon Chaney, Jr., Carole — and Victor Mature — won't talk.

Mr. Martin, who contributed his technical genius to the picture reincarnation of these animated models, Mr. Martin continues to say that many believers that dinosaurs died because they were allergic to volcanic grasses

For, he explains, "I don't suggest it as the sole cause of the dinosaurs sudden extinction, but it may have been an important contribution.

"The explanations thus far advanced account for the extinction of the world's most peculiar creatures. There had been..."

And now comes Antone Martin with the most sensational theory of all. He has a theory to explain the dinosaurs died because they were allergic to volcanic grasses.

A word about Martin. He is a man who carved out his career with a jackknife. He is a whittler of note.

"I've had a knife in my hands since I can remember," he says. "I began to make a practice of carving subjects was animals. My interest in geology and paleontology was born when I began a scientific course of study at U.C.L.A. I was given a scientific ability to some practical use when I found that it helped me to model the extinct animals at the University of California at Los Angeles. To illustrate a point, whittled a prehistoric animal for my classes. My professors at U.C.L.A. saw it and commended me for its scientific accuracy.

land, and grasses to birds, leaves and condition that protected them from hungry predators. Again, insects carried the pollen about. Their hiding places excluded dust and gas until resistance could be

The dinosaurs were allergic to dust and gas. They died from those who succumbed and those who survived. But science has learned today. But science has learned that if another element, aluminum, is present in the dust, you have silica results. The amount of silica necessary to kill, or the amount of diatomaceous earth necessary, is so small as to be immeasurable. Also this fact has been definitely noted that men who work in dusty mines for a lifetime without serious result, other-wise succumb to silicosis within a few months in the same mines. The latter have no resistance. This leads to the conviction that it is those who are more delicate, less able to resist bad conditions than the more rugged, die out.

Thus, Martin theorizes, the dinosaurs died. Imposing, formidable beasts they were, yet they had their weaklings. Some men can resist disease conditions that kill others. Nature has a drastic way of dealing with her weaklings.

The Biggest Thrill in a Million Years!

VICTOR MATURE as the "CAVE MAN"

Like most films, *One Million B.C.* was released under a few different titles. In Britain, it was released as *Man and His Mate* and was supposedly edited to remove shots of animal cruelty. Supposedly there also existed a cut of the film called *The Cave Dwellers* that removed the modern scenes that bookended the story. The film was released in Canada as *Tumak, Son of the Jungle* while in Italy it was *In the Path of Monsters*. In 1952 it was rereleased in the U.S. as *Cave Man*. Other alternate versions of *B.C.* include TV cuts, which, according to Don Glut, often removed many of the picture's exciting scenes. The baby triceratops, the cave bear, and the glyptodont were sometimes victims of time constraints. Oddly, the modern-day bookends were always retained!

CINETONE FILMS présente

Victor MATURE
Carole LANDIS

TUMAK
fils de la Jungle

avec LON CHANEY Jr.
mise en scène HAL ROACH

DE STRIJD OM HET LEVEN

CASTLE FILMS

PRESENTS

One Million B.!

COPYRIGHT MCMLIII BY UNITED WORLD FILMS
THEATRICAL AND TELEVISION RIGHTS RESERVED
ALL FOREIGN RIGHTS RESERVED

BATTLE OF THE GIANTS
FROM "ONE MILLION B.C."

RUNNING TIME: 8:15 (24 FPS)
TELEVISION AND THEATRICAL RIGHTS RESERVED

UNIVERSAL 8 FILMS

SUPER 200 SERIES

WHITE MAGNETIC SOUND EDITION

With the dawn of man's intelligence, he learned to communicate —

— to provide a stable food supply —

— to band together facing the terrors of nature

This early brotherhood enabled man to survive and to progress

BATTLE OF THE GIANTS

Gigantic PREHISTORIC DINOSAURS are shown in a battle to the death as cavemen watch, terrified. The prehistoric days come alive again as the unearthly monsters engage each other in battle.

One Million B.C. received two 8-minute digest versions from Castle Films on 8mm. One focused on the "dinosaurs" and was called "Battle of the Giants." The other was called "1 Million B.C." and offered a digest version of the climax. Screengrabs of that version can be seen to the left.

BATTLE of the GIANTS

AFTER ONE MILLION B.C.

Despite being a huge hit in 1940, *B.C.* oddly didn't spawn a host of imitators. But, this could have been due to WWII, which was raging at the time. Caveman pictures wouldn't begin to make a resurgence until the 1950s, when monster movies and dinosaurs in film became popular. In fact, *B.C.* was part of the prehistoric wave, as it was re-released in 1952 under the title of *Cave Man*.

That same year saw the release of Mexico's *The Beautiful Dreamer*. The 75 minute comedy is a bit similar to *The Flintstones*, which it predates by nearly ten years. Many of the Flintstones gags are there, such as chiseling a stone newspaper, bowling with rocks, eating dinosaurs as though they were chicken, etc.

Clearly a spoof of *B.C.*, the film mostly takes place in the prehistoric past but is bookended by modern segments.

A group of archeologists finds a perfectly preserved caveman that has been sleeping in his cave for 10,000 years. The caveman doesn't tell them that, however. Somehow, much like the magic archeologist in *B.C.*, the main professor is able to perfectly narrate the caveman's story.

Right away we are treated to shots of the prehistoric past. A volcano, another image evocative of *B.C.*, is placed in the center of the landscape. Two stopmotion brontosaurs drink from a pool in a swamp, while from a rocky overhang a stegosaurus utters an uncharacteristic growl at his fellow herbivores. The stegosaurus puppet amusingly awakens our sleeping protagonist, the caveman Triki-tran.

A tyrannosaurus comes along to terrorize the stegosaur puppet, and a nice little battle takes place. It's fake as all get out, of course, but if you like old fashioned miniatures and effects, it's a fun sequence. These aren't the last of the dinos either, they pop up sporadically throughout the rest of the film. In one scene, they even dance!

Lobby Card for *The Beautiful Dreamer* (1952).

The film's story harkens back to the silent era caveman films, which often had two cavemen fighting over the same woman, which is the case here. It also precedes elements of *When Dinosaurs Ruled the Earth* (1970). In that film, prehistoric religious zealots pursue a girl named Sanna because they believe she is the cause of recent atmospheric phenomena. In this film, there are two different tribes, one of which worships fire and the other of which worships water. Naturally, they don't get along. And naturally, Triki-tran, a member of the Fire Tribe, falls in love with a girl from the Water Tribe.

The prehistoric portion of the film ends with a volcanic eruption around forty minutes in. This is accomplished partially through archival footage of a real nighttime eruption. There is also new special effects footage that shows our poor dinosaur pals getting swallowed into the earth. This all happens right after Triki-tran has been drugged

by an enemy who steals his bride. It is also this magical potion that knocked him out and somehow managed to preserve him for thousands of years.

The rest of the film concerns Triki-tran's adventures in the present, learning to dance and speak Spanish. In the modern world he meets a woman who is the reincarnation of his lost love. At the picture's end, just as she is about to marry a rival suitor, an earthquake strikes. She has a flashback to the prehistoric past and remembers that Triki-tran is her true love. The two get back together, and it's a happy ending (except for the jilted fiancé).

All in all, *The Beautiful Dreamer* is a forgotten trailblazer of a film in certain, small ways. Technically, it was the first of a subgenre wherein a caveman is revived in the modern day. It's floating around online, though it's not subtitled. But, it's still funny even if you can't understand the dialogue.

that would continue with *Eegah* (1962) and *Trog* (1970) among others.

1961's *Valley of the Dragons* resurrected not only the caveman concept, but also footage from *B.C.* As it was, the 1940 film had lived on for many years due to the fact that the movie's b-roll footage and alternate takes were sold off to a stock footage company. Therefore, whenever someone needed a quick dinosaur scene they would purchase the *B.C.* footage and off they went. The effects footage from the film was used in dozens of other movies. It's unknown just how many films for sure the *B.C.* footage ended up in, but on the next page there's a partial filmography.

Top: Still from *Dinosaurus!* (1960) Bottom: Poster for *Teenage Caveman* (1958).

One of the first major American features to return viewers to the Stone Age was *Teenage Caveman* (1958). It was shot under the title of *Prehistoric World*, but was rechristened due to the success of movies like *I Was a Teenage Werewolf*. The movie has an interesting twist in that we only think it takes place in the prehistoric past, but a surprise twist reveals it's a post-apocalyptic future wherein mankind has reverted to the Stone Age.

Dinosaurus! (1960) brought the co-existing dinosaurs and caveman into the modern era. In the story, a frozen brontosaurus, tyrannosaurus, and a Neanderthal are thawed out on a tropical island. Though it wasn't the first, the film helped to popularize the "caveman revives in modern times" subgenre

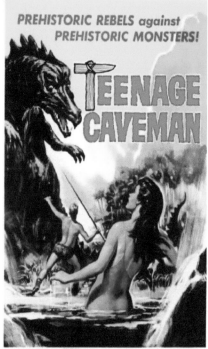

PREHISTORIC REBELS *against* PREHISTORIC MONSTERS!

TEENAGE CAVEMAN

ROBERT VAUGHN · DARRAH MARSHALL · LESLIE BRADLEY · Produced & Directed by ROGER CORMAN
Screenplay by R. WRIGHT CAMPBELL · A JAMES H. NICHOLSON and SAMUEL Z. ARKOFF Production · An AMERICAN INTERNATIONAL Picture

Tarzan's Desert Mystery (1943) U.S./B&W/70m. Tarzan and Boy trek through a mysterious desert full of prehistoric life to find the cure to jungle fever. This may have been the first film to use the *B.C.* stock footage in the form of the lizard fight. It occurs near the end of the film. Though Tarzan and dinosaurs may seem strange to moviegoers, in the books he tangled with dinosaurs semi-often. No new dinosaur effects were created to my memory, but a giant spider was. **Starring:** Johnny Weissmuller, Nancy Kelly, Johnny Sheffield **Director:** William Thiele

Jungle Manhunt (1951) U.S. /B&W/65m. Jungle Jim helps a freelance photographer find a missing WWII vet in the jungle. Though the *B.C.* footage had been used in a few Superman serials and short films since *Tarzan's Desert Mystery*, in 1951, Weissmuller again encountered the wrestling *B.C.* lizards to less excitement. An Allosaurus costume was constructed to fight Jungle Jim too. Supposedly the footage was shot and then dropped, meaning *B.C.* constitutes this film's only dino scenes. **Starring:** Johnny Weissmuller, Sheila Ryan, Bob Waterfield **Director:** Lew Landers

Two Lost Worlds (1951) U.S. /B&W/63m. Two rival suitors must rescue the object of their affection from pirates before being stranded on an island of dinosaurs. This movie is half pirate adventure and half lost world/dinosaur movie. Even its pirate footage is taken from other films! Not only are *B.C.*'s lizards pressed into service, so is its volcano which serves as the film's climax. **Starring:** James Arness, Laura Elliot, William Kennedy **Director:** Norman Dawn

Untamed Women (1952) U.S. /B&W/70m. A pilot crashes in a land ruled over by prehistoric women. Like *Two Lost Worlds*, the amount of *B.C.* footage ran high and included the volcanic climax. **Starring:** Mikel Conrad, Doris Merrick **Director:** W. Merle Connor

Robot Monster (1953) U.S. /B&W/62m. An alien invader terrorizes a family on a picnic. One of the most notorious features of all time, *Robot Monster* borrowed dino scenes not only from *B.C.*, but *Lost Continent* (1951) as well. The dinosaurs are reanimated to destroy the earth, by the way. **Starring:** George Nader, Claudia Barrett **Director:** Phil Tucker

King Dinosaur (1955) U.S. /B&W/63m. Explorers on Planet Nova encounter a tyrannosaurs rex... which is really an iguana. Surprisingly, the *B.C.* footage is minimal and makes use of the mammoth, the glyptodont, and only a few lizard shots. The iguana footage shot for the film was mostly brand new, but still awful. **Starring:** Bill Bryant, Wanda Curtis, Douglas Henderson **Director:** Bert I. Gordon

She Demons (1958) U.S./B&W /77m. Shipwrecked survivors face off against an island of deformed Nazi experiments... of which there are no dinosaurs, only the titular She Demons. In this case, a few shots of *B.C.*'s volcano/earthquake footage was used to help end the film on a bang. **Starring:** Irish McCalla, Tod Griffin, Victor Sen Yung **Director:** Richard E. Cunha

Teenage Caveman (1958) U.S./ B&W/65m. Teenage survivors encounter mutant creatures resembling dinosaurs in a post-apocalyptic wasteland. The dinosaurs in this case were again brought to life via outtakes from *B.C.*, as well as one shot from *Unknown Island* (1948). **Starring:** Robert Vaughn, Darrah Marshall **Director:** Roger Corman

***The Incredible Petrified World* (1960) U.S./B&W/70m.** Oceanic explorers become trapped in an underwater cavern with a madman. No dinosaurs in this one, but there is a volcano. This is where the *B.C.* footage, really just a few shots, comes into play. **Starring:** John Carradine, George Skaff, Sheila Noonan **Director:** Jerry Warren

***Valley of the Dragons* (1961) U.S./B&W/79m.** Two men become stranded on a comet full of prehistoric life (basically). This film hinged on *B.C.*'s footage more so than any other, and not just the outtakes sold to stock footage libraries, but every piece of footage in *B.C.* (one of the producers had the rights). Therefore, this movie's climax basically is *B.C.* all over again with new actors edited into the proceedings. **Starring:** Cesare Danova, Sean McClory **Director:** Edward Bernds

***Adventure at the Center of the Earth* (1965) Mexico/B&W/85m.** Explorers search out prehistoric life in a deep cavern. Anyone who knows *Gigantis, the Fire Monster* (1959) will recall a famous scene where the history of the world is recreated via a diverse array of dinosaur footage. The same thing happens in this film, wherein experts watch a film reel full of clips from *B.C.*, *Unknown Island*, and *Beautiful Dreamer*. The monsters they find within the cavern are all anthropomorphic bat and lizard men. **Starring:** Kitty de Hoyos,

Javier Solís **Director:** Alfredo B. Crevenna

***One Million AC/DC* (1969) U.S./Color/80m.** This horrid soft-core porn spoof *of One Million Years B.C.* (1966) uses the infamous *B.C.* lizard scene but at least had some new (but awful) footage filmed of a T-rex. **Starring:** Susan Berkely, Billy Wolf, Sharon Wells **Director:** Ed De Priest

***Horror of the Blood Monsters* (1970) U.S./Color/85m.** Explorers trace the source of a vampire plague on earth to a distant planet and go there to find a cure. To make use of all the *B.C.* B&W stock footage, the planet's atmosphere has a strange tint to it, so as to tint the *B.C.* footage the same color in this case. **Starring:** John Carradine, Robert Dix **Director:** Al Adamson

***Tarzan the Mighty Man* (1974) Turkey/B&W/70m.** This un-authorized Turkish Tarzan was wisely shot in B&W, not just to reuse the *B.C.* footage but shots from numerous other films as well, like 1938's *Tarzan's Revenge* starring Glenn Morris in the role. Even Weissmuller's famous yell is used in this film. **Starring:** Yavuz Selekman **Director:** Kunt Tulgar

***Aadi Yug* (1978) India/Color/ 106m.** This Bollywood quasi-remake of the *B.C.* films was one of the last of its kind to reuse the old *B.C.* footage in all seriousness. It also illegally used some footage from *Frankenstein Conquers the World* (1965). It's the usual story of caveman looking for cavewoman, just a bit more meandering and with dance numbers. **Starring:** Mehndi Jamal, Vinay Kumar **Director:** Prasad

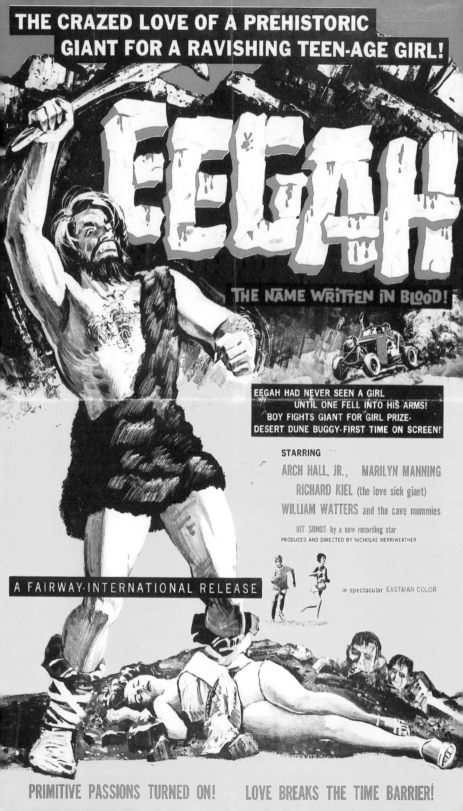

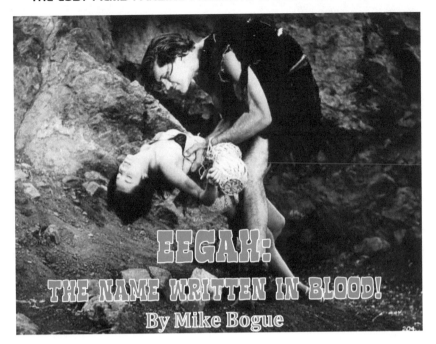

EEGAH: THE NAME WRITTEN IN BLOOD!
By Mike Bogue

In 1973, the ad tagline for George Lucas's *American Graffiti* was, "Where were you in '62?" No doubt some denizens of that bygone year were at the drive-in, and some of them were probably watching 1962's *Eegah*, a low-budget production from Fairway International. The film chronicles the tale of a somehow still-alive caveman who cavorts with the California cast until his inevitable demise.

Some might be tempted to call the production "prehistoric" in terms of not just its title character, but also its film technique. Indeed, many consider it one of the worst films ever made. For example, *Rotten Tomatoes* gives it a "fresh" rating of 0% out of eight reviews. Certainly the movie is no winner, and yet . . .

Richard Kiel, years before fame as "Jaws" in 1977's *The Spy Who Loved Me* and 1979's *Moonraker*, portrays Eegah. The movie never adequately explains what this caveman is doing alive in the 20th century; the heroine's father opines that the sulfur in Eegah's cave has kept him young all these years. Naturally. So why hasn't anyone seen him before the heroine literally runs into him with her sports car? Again, the film's explanation lacks credibility, and reminds one of the similarly insufficient rationale for the giant arachnid's sudden appearance in 1958's *Earth vs. the Spider*.

Much of the film takes place in Eegah's cave, where Eegah holds Roxy (Marilyn Manning) and her father Mr. Miller (Arch Hall Sr.) captive. Here the movie often strives for comedy, such as Roxy sickened by sulfur water, pretending she is talking to Eegah's mummified relatives, and giving Eegah a shave (no, I'm not kidding), in which he licks shaving cream and squirts it on his face (maybe he's a relative of Larry, Moe, and Curly?). But it's also clear Eegah has other plans for the heroine, and here the movie becomes uncomfortable.

Tom (Arch Hall Jr.), the hero, helps rescue Roxy (his girlfriend of course) and her father from the smitten caveman. Strangely, they choose not to tell anyone about Eegah, the heroine's father claiming that authorities would take him away to turn him into a lab exhibit. But of course, we haven't seen the last of this caveman whose name is written in blood.

Eegah is portrayed as a semi-tragic character—not unlike Universal's Gill Man, Eegah is a stranger in a strange land. The 7 foot, 2 inch Kiel gives a lively performance, and his overdubbed caveman grunts and groans prove effective, somewhat recalling Paul Frees' vocals for 1957's *The Cyclops*. Naturally, in the finale the caveman goes in search of the heroine, and is killed by law officers. Roxy and her father express the usual ritual sadness over his inevitable demise.

The movie scores a few points for imagination. For example, Eegah's aforementioned desiccated relatives are a nice idea, and he talks to them as though he thinks they are still alive. The opening credits, though undeniably cheap, resonate with a crude inventiveness. Indeed, the movie evokes the undeniable feel of drive-in movies of the 1960s, and as such has a certain cockeyed charm for hopeless nostalgia addicts such as myself.

Although credits say the movie was produced and directed by Nicholas Merriwether, this was actually a pseudonym for Arch Hall Sr.—the film's hero Tom is Mr. Hall's son, Arch Hall Jr. Hall Sr. participated in various functions on a number of 1960's low-budget films. His son Hall Jr. appeared infrequently; probably his best-known film is 1963's *The Sadist*, in which he stars as a psychotic killer. This one gets 2 ½ stars from Leonard Maltin, who found Hall Jr.'s performance "distressingly believable."

Well, it's pretty safe to say no one will find anything "distressingly believable" about *Eegah*. But therein lies its appeal, what there is of it. No doubt twentysomethings would be stunned to hear old guys like myself actually paid money to see movies like this. But we did. Of course, I can't blame others if they're not eegah to see this one. But if you could withstand that previous pun without throwing this magazine across the room, *Eegah* might be right up your retro alley.

***

Mike Bogue is the author of such books as Atomic Drive-In *and* Apocalypse Then: American and Japanese Atomic Cinema, 1951-1967.

WANTED!
MORE INFORMATION ON UNMADE MOVIES LIKE
FIVE BILLION B.C.!

Before Hammer remade *One Million B.C.* in 1966, Edward G. Ulmer (director of 1934's *The Black Cat*) planned to make a prehistoric epic called *Five Billion B.C.* This is all according to Mark Berry's *The Dinosaur Filmography*, and the project is listed as being in development around 1960. Very little is known about it other than the fact that it was never finished. Jim Danforth recalled to Berry that he did some storyboards for the project, but that was it.

We don't know exactly what it is, where it is now, but in the 1950s Japan produced some sort of caveman movie. It was titled *Human History of 500,000 Years*, which I suppose could translate to *500,000 B.C.* The director's name listed as Miyachi. Another source identified it as possibly being a Japanese poster for a French film from Nouvelles Éditions de Films.

Thanks to Niels Petter Solberg for finding the poster on page opposite (and the bottom two images), as well as Jolyon Yates and Kevin Mendorf for both finding the image to the right.

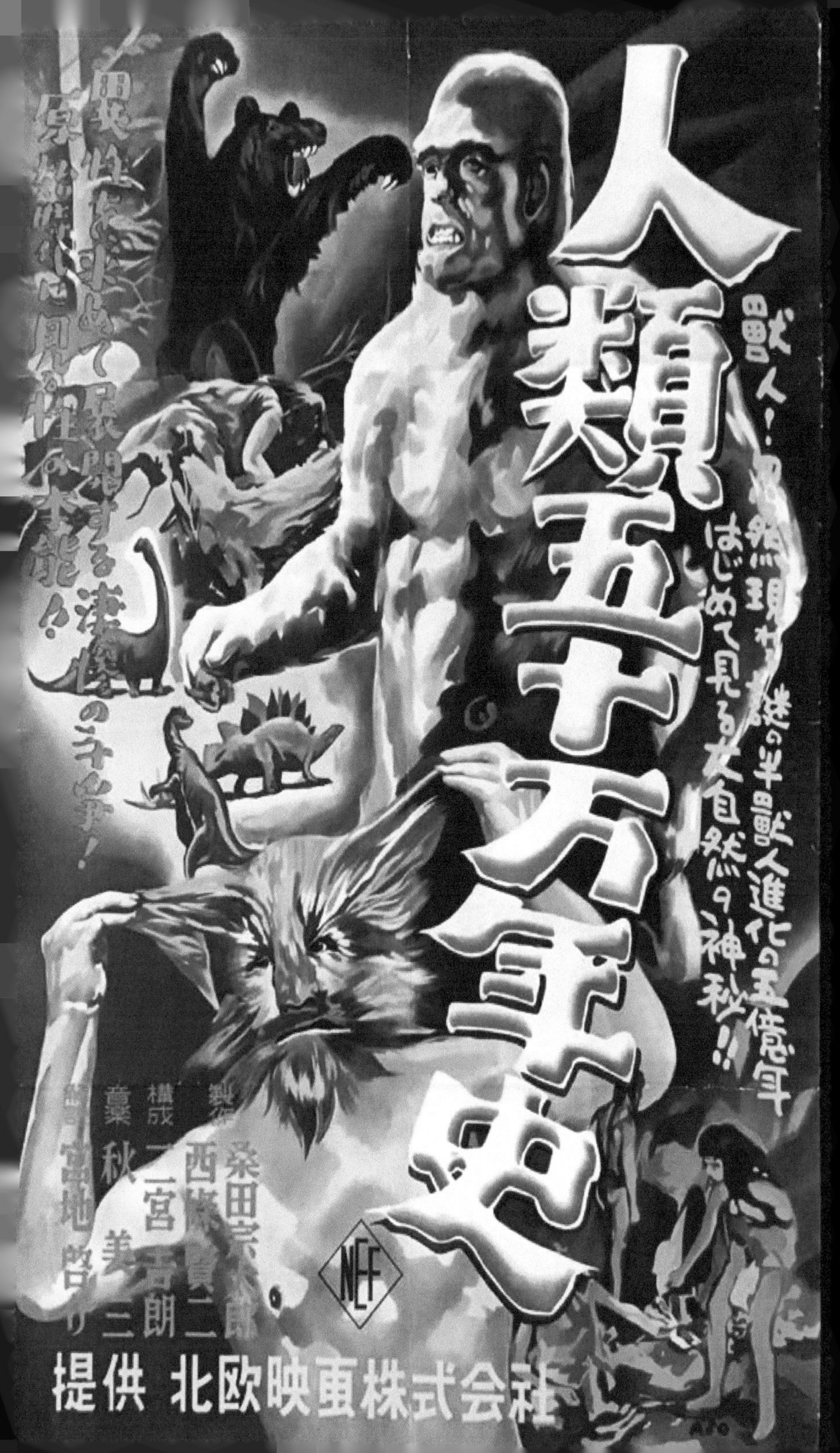
人類五十万年史
はじめて見る大自然の神秘!!
製作 桑田宗
構成 西
NEF
提供 北欧映画株式会社

THE MAMMOTH ONE FOR 1966

In the 1960s, Hammer was famous for their horror output more than anything else. Though they produced the odd adventure movie here and there, they didn't strike it big in that genre until they remade *She* in 1965 with Ursula Andress. Encouraged by the success of *She*, Michael Carreras was inspired to follow it up with another epic. Specifically, Carreras wanted to do something that was more appealing to families.

MILLION B.C.

This could result in higher grosses due to a broader appeal. His first thought was to do a giant monster movie, and since he had remade Merian C. Cooper's *She*, he decided that next he would remake *King Kong*. (This is interesting, as Cooper made *She* after *King Kong* and hoped that it would equal *Kong's* success. It didn't).

Director: Don Chaffey *Script*: Michael Carreras *SPFX Director*: Ray Harryhausen *Music*: Mario Nascimbene *Cast*: John Richardson (Tumak) Raquel Welch (Loana) Robert Brown (Akhoba) Martine Beswick (Nupondi) Percy Herbert (Sakana) *Release Date*: December 30, 1966 *Runtime*: 100 Minutes

Plot: Tumak, a brave hunter from the Rock Tribe, is cast out by his father Akhoba. Tumak wanders the desert and is found near death by the lovely Loana, of the peaceful Shell Tribe. Meanwhile, Tumak's brother, Sakana, has taken control of the Rock Tribe. When Tumak returns home with Loana, he takes back control of the tribe from Sakana. After a deadly earthquake, the survivors of the Rock and Shell tribes form a new tribe.

Though it's hard to imagine anyone else in the role, the original choice for Loana was Ursula Andress. Supposedly, shots of Loana emerging from the water were meant to be evocative of Andress's famous entrance as Honey Rider in *Dr. No* (1962). Ironically, the same voice actress, Nikki Van der Zyl, who dubbed Andress in *She* would end up dubbing Loana because Welch came down with tonsillitis while filming in the Canary Islands. The poster at right notably renamed the film *Loana*. Following Pages: Tom Chantrell's concept art. © 1966 Hammer Film Productions, Ltd. All Rights Reserved.

(*cont'd from page 29*) However, when Hammer went to RKO they were informed that the studio only leased the character for sequels, like the upcoming *King Kong Escapes* (1967), but not remakes.

So, it was back to the drawing board for Carreras and Hammer's looming "100th Production" (this was just a publicity ploy, Hammer's 100th production was already behind them and had not been a big event film). There are conflicting reports as to who it was who came up with the idea of remaking 1940's

SPECTACLE THAT WILL AMAZE YOU!

One Million B.C. Some imply that it was Carreras's idea, as he loved the combination of sex appeal and dinosaurs. More reputable accounts say that it was Kenneth Hyman of Seven-Arts who instigated this remake just as he did with *She*.

In fact, the idea was to repeat *She's* success by reteaming Ursula Andress and John Richardson. Andress wasn't interested though, and later the *B.C.* remake's director, Don Chaffey, made the comment that he hoped to find some unknowns to play the lead roles. While John Richardson did return from *She*, and certainly wasn't unknown, neither was Raquel Welch. She had just come off of the hit feature *Fantastic Voyage* (1966).

With Welch and Richardson providing more sex appeal than the original, Carreras also knew that he didn't want his dinosaurs to be giant lizards. He was keenly aware of the stopmotion work of the great Ray Harryhausen, and approached him about the project. Though Harryhausen was no fan of the original (due to its use of lizards), he, too, came to realize that the picture had potential for a remake.

Our first inklings of abandoned concepts come from the wonderful art of Hammer's favorite poster artist, Tom Chantrell. The talented artist did several concept drawings to help drum up interest in the film, though it's uncertain if Carreras ever considered some of the scenes he envisioned, such as a Kronosaurus chasing cave people under the water.

For certain, a mammoth was meant to be in the film at one point (a mammoth had appeared in the original *B.C.*). A script from July of 1965 had it slated to be the first creature that Tumak would encounter in the wild, which was also the case in the original.

Supposedly, the idea was dropped because Hammer didn't want to trouble themselves working with a real elephant draped in fur. It's unknown if it was ever considered for Harryhausen's stopmotion technique either. Other sources simply say Hammer felt a wooly mammoth wasn't fantastic enough for the feature.

As many will no doubt remember, the first creature Tumak encounters in this version is a giant iguana. This idea was two-fold, as it provided a quick nod to the original, and Harryhausen felt it would make the stopmotion dinosaurs look better when they appeared later.

Among other cut critters were giant scorpions, which Harryhausen would famously animate in *Clash of the Titans* (1981). It's unknown if they were to be in place of or in addition to the giant spider. In either case, like the spider, they would be enlarged via rear projection rather than animation just like the spider.

At the start of production, Harryhausen storyboarded three major set-pieces that were to shape the film. First up was the Allosaurus attack, which Harryhausen stated was a tyrannosaur in one early draft. The sequence was meant to take place in a swamp in one early version as well. As the scene evolved, Harryhausen had a different entrance in mind for the Allosaurus. He wanted its arrival preceded by a giant prehistoric bird, the phororhacus, which appeared in his *Mysterious Island* (1961).

Specifically, the bird was kept in a pen by the Shell People. Loana goes inside to fetch one of its gigantic eggs, and it bounds out the gate. When it escapes, Tumak and Loana chase it down only for it to be pounced

Some of the *B.C.* remake's famous scenes descended from an unmade dinosaur movie called *Creation* from 1930. That film was replaced by *King Kong* by RKO, and the dinosaur models built for *Creation* were used on *Kong*. The main image is concept art from *Creation* showing a pterodactyl carrying off a woman, which inspired a similar scene in *B.C.* The Arsinotherium (inset, top) was another holdover from *Creation* that Harryhausen tried to bring into *B.C.* Harryhausen recalled Hammer axed the Arsinotherium because it "wasn't prehistoric enough." Harryhausen would try several more times to insert an Arsinotherium into his pictures (notably, Trog was to fight one in *Sinbad and the Eye of the Tiger*). The concept art of the Brontosaurus attacking some of the characters from *Creation* (inset, bottom) inspired a similar scene for *B.C.* that would itself be axed.

upon by the Allosaurus. Harryhausen used this idea with an Ornithomimus in *Valley of Gwangi* (1969) instead.

Then there was the famous pterodactyl scene, where Loana is carried away and almost eaten by one of the prehistoric reptiles. The inspiration for the scene actually came from the original screenplay for *King Kong*. It was titled *The Beast*, and was penned by Edgar Wallace. In the scene, a pterodactyl was intended to pluck a man from the ground and drop him into its nest to feed its young. Though Harryhausen remembered the scene from *The Beast/King Kong*, it actually originated even further back in *Creation* (1930). The scene in *Creation* had a pterodactyl abducting the heroine, who is saved when the hero swings from a vine to kick the flying reptile, causing it to drop his lady love.

The third set-piece represented the film's original ending, which didn't make it into the picture in any form or fashion. It had a brontosaurus attacking the cavepeople.

On image:
ASSOCIATED BRITISH-PATHE PRESENTS
A HAMMER FILM PRODUCTION
"ONE MILLION YEARS B.C." (A)
starring
RAQUEL WELCH JOHN RICHARDSON
with
PERCY HERBERT ROBERT BROWN
MARTINE BESWICK
TECHNICOLOR
RELEASED THROUGH WARNER-PATHE DISTRIBUTORS LTD

Using stills shot for the axed, alternate ending, Hammer created this exciting publicity still that shows what the ending would've looked like had Harryhausen animated it. © 1966 Hammer Film Productions, Ltd.

(It's possible Chantrell came up with the scene depending on who did their artwork first considering it was one of his concept posters).

The Brontosaurus scene went through several iterations. An early script dated May 21, 1965, had the Brontosaurus attack the cave of the Shell Tribe, but in the next script it was revised to become the Rock Tribe. Though everyone was aware that the Brontosaur wasn't carnivorous, it was decided that the long snake-like neck made it a compelling opponent. (Besides, they had already tussled with a carnivorous theropod earlier) The dinosaur would've used its long neck to reach into a cave and pluck out a poor caveman (this idea, too, Harryhausen admitted came from

1930's aborted *Creation*). The others it would trample underfoot.

It's a shame the scene was cut, as it sounds fantastic. It would've ended with Tumak and his tribesmen backing the Brontosaurs onto a rocky bridge over a volcanic chasm. The rock formation would collapse under the creature's weight, and it would plunge into the lava. There was also an alternative means of death wherein the cavemen cause an avalanche that buries the Brontosaur under tons of rock.

As to why it was cut, Carreras felt the movie was getting too long and had too many action scenes (if you'll recall, the British version was 100 minutes. Back then, producers wanted features to be shorter

Harryhausen's storyboard for the Brontosaurus scene (above) and his envisioned concept for the film's poster (left). Opposite page: Storyboards for the brontosaur scene.

because they were often double billed.)

Rear projection plates of the actors were shot on location, and John Richardson confirmed in an interview with Mark Mawston in *Cinema Retro* #46 that, "I remember acting out on what's on those stills at that location." [pp.11]

Though the Brontosaur battle was always slated to be followed by an eruption (perhaps the Brontosaur's plunge into the lava caused the eruption?) Carreras rewrote the ending on location to more greatly emphasize the cataclysm. Preceding the eruption, he also added in the fight between the two tribes, so that was a last minute addition.

BRONTOSAURUS SEQUENCE   1.

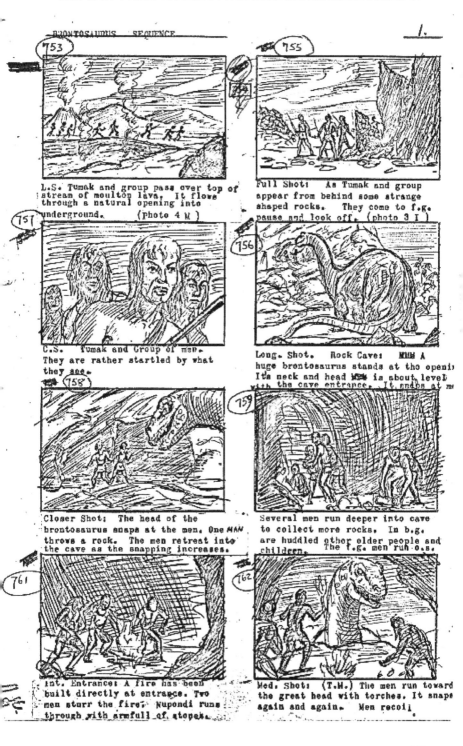

753

L.S. Tumak and group pass over top of
stream of moulton lava. It flows
through a natural opening into
underground.   (Photo 4 M)

755

Full Shot: As Tumak and group
appear from behind some strange
shaped rocks.   They come to f.g.
pause and look off. (photo 3 I)

757

C.S.   Tumak and Group of men.
They are rather startled by what
they see.

756

Long. Shot.   Rock Cave: A
huge brontosaurus stands at the openi;
It's neck and head is about level
with the cave entrance. It snaps at m

758

Closer Shot: The head of the
brontosaurus snaps at the men. One MAN
throws a rock.   The men retreat into
the cave as the snapping increases.

759

Several men run deeper into cave
to collect more rocks. In b.g.
are huddled other older people and
children.   The f.g. men run O.s.

761

Int. Entrance: A fire has been
built directly at entrance. Two
men stırr the fire; Nupondi runs
through with armfull of stones.

762

Med. Shot: (T.M.) The men run toward
the great head with torches. It snaps
again and again.   Men recoil

37

This storyboard implies an alternate version of the story where Tumak is found in the water, much like Victor Mature in the original *B.C.* It also appears as though the turtle intends to eat him!

Harryhausen greatly lamented the excision of the brontosaur battle. "I regret that the sequence was never completed," he wrote in his book *Ray Harryhausen: An Animated Life.* As Harryhausen put it, "with its long neck and tail, [the Brontosaurus] lends itself so perfectly to animation and provides the potential for so many exciting movements."

As for the end cataclysm itself, its final shots were envisioned a bit differently as well. One imagined closing shot, perhaps meant to be evocative of current nuclear fears, would have shown the survivors marching towards a huge mushroom cloud created by the eruption.

Other changes to the movie's development mirrored the struggles of the original *B.C.* in terms of how to tell the story in the absence of traditional dialogue. If you'll recall, back in 1940, D.W. Griffith wanted all of his version of *B.C.* narrated. Ironically, Hammer almost did the same thing. *Last Bus to Bray* (a special publication from *Little Shoppe of Horrors*) implies that David Kossoff recorded narration to guide the viewer through the film's full 100 minute runtime! *Last Bus to Bray* described it as "unconventional" and that it was "more like a junior wildlife documentary". Instead, Hammer hired Robert Beatty to do a shorter, more straightforward narration to kick off the film.

Although the movie was eventually filmed in the Canary Islands, initially Carreras was

Above: This test image from *One Million Years B.C.* (labeled Mutt and Jeff by Harryhausen) shows the Allosaurus and the Ceratosaurus against the background used for the earthquake scenes. As you can see, the two models are the same size, even though the Ceratosaurus is presented as being quite large in comparison to the Allosaurus in the film. Bottom right: The fight between the Ceratosaurus and the Triceratops was supposed to end with blood oozing from the loser's "gaping wound" but that was deemed too bloody and so was decided against. © 1966 Hammer Film Productions, Ltd. All Rights Reserved.

thinking of filming it amidst the volcanic rocks of Iceland in widescreen. Due to issues of limited daylight and sun, Iceland was nixed. Instead, Harryhausen, Carreras, and Chaffey fell in love with the island Lanzarote in the Canary Islands when they saw it and decided that had to be the locale. As to the aspect ratio, Harryhausen argued that widescreen would be too difficult.

What do you think of all those ideas? A version of *B.C.* shot in Iceland. One in which the entire picture is explained by an unseen narrator like a "junior wildlife documentary." It's also a version that ends with a Brontosaurus battle and the survivors marching off into an even more uncertain future. Apart from the missing Brontosaurus scene, I'd say the finished version of *B.C.* was the preferable one.

Audiences agreed. It was exactly the big hit that Hammer had hoped for. And it needed to be considering it was Hammer's highest budgeted feature ever at 422,000 pounds! Naturally, the film's success would lead to many imitators and a few follow-ups, made and unmade alike...

The beautiful Raquel Welch often suggested ways to make her character a bit more nuanced, which director Don Chaffey usually dismissed.

PRESSBOOK

20th CENTURY FOX

| WEATHER FAIR 60's 150's near the volcano. t'm'w: Glacier |

THE BC ☒ NEWS

1 KAYDNIT
OR
2 FRAILINS

POST HERALD DISPATCH AND FRUMKIN

Vol. 1   1,000,000 Years B.C.

BEAUTY KIDNAPPED BY WINGED MONSTER ONE MILLION YEARS B.C.

Prehistoric Civilization Up In Arms!

(B.C. Rock-Photo)   A Savage Pteradactyl Kidnaps The Beautiful Raquel Welch In One Of The Exciting Scenes From The New Twentieth Century-Fox Release, One Million Years B.C. The Vivacious Miss Welch Is Constantly Being Followed By Strangers, But The Pteradactyl Incident Was Something Of A First.

"One Million Years B.C."
Stones Them At The Cave Theatre!

SCIENTIFIC BREAKTHROUGH!

Grommet Gridgin aims the spear he has just invented as scoffers watch. The scoffers hint that he was really trying to invent the toothpick but got carried away. In any case, this is certainly a boon to mankind. No longer will we have to suffer the fist fight, the hair pulling match, the stone throwing match. Now for the first time man can hope for something better. He can wage full scale war! Ah, progress.

Fur Is "In" This Spring

The voluptuous Raquel Welch models the original fur bikini, a dyed brontosaurus featuring a low neckline and a hem that plunges two inches below the grilsk. It's the latest in high fashion. Well ... maybe it's not so "high" but it's fashion. What can you expect from a bunch of neanderthals!

WEDDING BELLS?

Tumak and Loana were seen getting cozy by the lava quarry last evening. This marks the second time in two nights they have been seen together. It's shameful the way kids are being brought up today.

Vincent Van Freebish Stands By His Latest Masterpiece

Our resident wall painter (he prefers the term artist) has just completed his master work. "I call it buffalos," he said. "I don't know why, it just reminds me of my mother." Vincent's big fear is that his contemporary work will not stand the test of time.

The entire population of 1,000,001 b.c. had a reunion, celebrating their making it through another year. Highlight of the evening came when Loana smashed Nupondi's head with a brick. Nice going Loana!

PREHISTORIC MONSTERS ROAM THE EARTH AGAIN IN
"One Million Years B.C."

"One Million Years B.C." is more than a rip roaring adventure film. It is extremely informative. As Raquel Welch fights her way through the remarkably realistic prehistoric landscape, she encounters beasts that give the layman and the student an excellent graphic picture of zoology, "One Million Years B.C."

Beast Against Beast For Survival
"One Million Years B.C."!

A savage triceratops (try-SERRA-tops) and a towering Ceratosaurus (Serra-tow-SAW-Russ) fight it out in "One Million Years B.C." Both dinosaurs lived in the jurassic period and were about twenty feet in length. The Triceratops is easily distinguished by his three horns and the armor plate guarding his soft neck. The Ceratosaurus, so called for the small horn on his snout, is the carnivorous (flesh-eating) cousin of the Tyranosaurus (Ty-ran-o-SAW-Russ).

Terror From The Skies!

The winged reptile, pteradactyl (Terra-DACK-till), was certainly one of the most menacing of creatures. This flying reptile, like its animal counterpart, the bat, had wings of skin stretched between long finger bones. Unlike the bat, the pteradactyl grew to tremendous size and was capable of devouring large life forms.

A 40 Ton Mountain Of Flesh With Just 4 Teeth

The Brontosaurus (Bron-tow-SAW-russ), or "Thunder Lizard," was a large and foreboding behemoth. Oddly, this moving mountain of flesh existed solely on soft wet vegetation. Feeding his forty tons of bulk was a very small head containing but four simple peg teeth. Still, the sight of this beast and the rumble of the earth beneath him, froze the hearts of man and every animal that lived. "One Million Years B.C."

GIANT CLEMMYS GUTTATA
(Klem-ees-goo-TA-ta) MENACES MAN
"ONE MILLION YEARS B.C."

This giant forerunner of the modern day sea turtle, weighed tons and had jaws powerful enough to snap large trees at their base and battle the most gigantic dinosaurs.

MONSTER MANIA MAGAZINE

The January, 1967, issue of Monster Mania is dedicated to a "Tribute to Hammer Issue." Its color cover catches, both on the front and back, the exciting spirit of "One Million Years B.C." the Seven Arts-Hammer production being released in De Luxe color by 20th Century-Fox. The magazine's Movie Review is a six-page illustrated feature on the motion picture. The 8 1/4" x 10 3/4" magazine has 68 pages devoted to Hammer productions and to such of the stars as Christopher Lee and Peter Cushing and director Terence Fisher. It retails for 35 cents per copy. For exhibitors, the magazine is available at 5 cents per copy and is a definite plus in exploitation of the picture. Please note that it will take about 10 days for delivery of your order. Please address orders to:

> Mr. Lee Irgang
> Renaissance Productions, Inc.
> 630 Spring Avenue
> Elkins Park, Penna.

POSTERS & ACCESSORIES

1 SHEET

24 SHEET

6 SHEET
WINDOW CARD

ALSO AVAILABLE

3-SHEET

40 x 60

30 x 40

22 x 28

INSERT CARD

SET OF (8) 11 x 14's

SET OF (6) 8 x 10 COLOR STILLS

SET OF B/W 8 x 10 STILLS

ONE MILLION YEARS B.C.

ONE MILLION YEARS B.C. UNCUT

For many years, in the U.S., the uncut version of *One Million Years B.C.* was a lost film. Due to different standards in entertainment, the U.S. version of *B.C.* was cut by 8 minutes. The first shot cut was of Tumak tearing off the tusk of the prehistoric boar, which was apparently considered too grotesque for U.S. audiences. Later, as the boar roasts in the cave of the rock tribe, an old man gets too close to the carcass. The cook tosses a rock into his head knocking him over.

Later, after the feast has been in progress for some time, Akhoba discards a bone with some flesh still attached. Two old men then wrestle over who gets to eat the scraps.

Tumak's trek through the desert was shortened by around one minute, removing some cool shots of him strolling past a prehistoric plant, a volcanic caldera, and some dinosaur bones.

Even the creature footage was subject to cuts, as the Archelon sequence runs almost one minute longer. In the cut shots, men of the Shell Tribe throw rocks at the giant turtle, and one attacks its shell from a hilltop.

Nupondi's wild dance in the cave, a sort of primitive wedding between her and Sakana, was shortened greatly, as it was considered risqué in America. Meanwhile, Tumak's exploration of the Shell Tribe's cave was cut down for being too boring perhaps. In the scene he examines their cave paintings and the paint they use to make them.

The Allosaurus sequence also fell victim to cuts, with a few shots of it menacing the young girl stuck in a tree removed. Tumak wrestling a spear away from a Shell man was cut before he runs off to face the beast, as were a few additional shots of Tumak circling the dinosaur.

The film's most famous deleted scene involved Tumak's second trip to the cave of the ape men. As he and Loana cower above them in a tree, they watch as the ape men fight. Portions of the fight exist in the U.S. cut, but not the scene where the loser gets its head bashed against a rock repeatedly. Off screen the man beast is beheaded, but we do see the severed head placed upon a stick.

The pterosaur scene is extended by over a minute. While it doesn't affect the plot, the missing shots are still interesting. It appears the scene was only shortened to tighten the pacing.

The end rumble between the two tribes is shortened. The U.S. cut lacked a scene of Sakana carrying Loana away. He tosses her off his shoulder to attack an enemy, and she seizes the opportunity to hit him with a rock. As for the end earthquake, numerous little snippets here and there are removed. In fact, the British and American cuts even tint the final shots in different ways (the British version is darker, the U.S. version is lighter with a bit more color).

CREATURES
THE WORLD
FORGOT

COLUMBIA PICTURES present HAMMER PRODUCTION

JULIE EGE/TONY BONNER/BRIAN O'SHAUGHNESSY
ROBERT JOHN·MICHAEL CARRERAS·DON CHAFFEY
TECHNICOLOR®

Hammer's success with *B.C.* would lead to two-quasi sequels and a continuation of the adventure-glamour movies that began with *She* in 1965. Of the two glamour movies there was *Prehistoric Women* (1967) and *Vengeance of She* (1968). The quasi-sequel to *B.C.*, *When Dinosaurs Ruled the Earth*, began to take shape in 1967, but wasn't released until 1970. Following that was a dinosaur-less quasi-*B.C.* remake entitled *Creatures the World Forgot* in 1971.

But that wasn't always the plan. Oddly enough, rather than announcing a "One Million Years B.C. II," Hammer announced a TV series based on the film instead in May of 1967! Hammer made repeated, unsuccessful attempts to find a financial backer for it up until late 1969, when they finally gave up.

According to *Hammer Complete: The Films, the Personnel, the Company* by Howard Maxford, Hammer first approached Twentieth Century-Fox about co-funding the series. This instead led to Hammer and Twentieth Century Fox to team up on a different series altogether: *Journey to the Unknown* (1968).

It's unknown how Hammer planned to bring the TV series dinosaurs to life, but perhaps it wouldn't have even featured dinosaurs, who knows? In that case, it would've been similar to *Creatures the World Forgot*, pictured above. Maybe Hammer would've used stock footage from *B.C.*'s dinosaurs from time to time? All we know, dinosaurs or no, is that the series would have been filmed in Antigua, an island in the West Indies.

Top Left: Poster for *Vengeance of She*. This film began alternatively as *She— Goddess of Love* and *Ayesha – Daughter of She*. Both iterations were meant for Ursula Andress, who turned them down. While John Richardson would return, many different replacements were considered for Andress. Among them were Susan Denberg (*Frankenstein Created Woman*), Samantha Jones, Britt Ekland, Sonja Romanoff, Camilla Sparv, Julie Kruger-Monsen, and Barbara Bouchet before Olinka Berova was cast. Don Sharp was the original choice for director, but was unavailable.   Right: Poster for *Prehistoric Women* which began as *Slave Girls of the White Rhino!*

The success of *B.C.* would inspire Ray Harryhausen to dust off a lost project of his mentor, Willis O'Brien. Simply titled *Gwangi*, it had been O'Brien's Cowboys vs. Dinosaurs fantasy. Harryhausen updated the original script, and produced the film with his usual production partner Charles H. Schneer. The production of the film would lead to Harryhausen being unavailable to work on Hammer's *When Dinosaurs Ruled the Earth*.

Harryhausen had apparently enjoyed his time at Hammer, because he pitched another project to them: a remake of 1933's *Deluge*. The film derived from a 1928 novel, set primarily in England, while the film relocated the nautical disasters to the U.S. The film was a precursor to the disaster movies of the 1970s.

It featured several earthquakes and an eclipse leading to a tidal wave demolishing New York.

Harryhausen's version would have had the tidal wave destroy London as in the novel. He pitched the project to Hammer immediately following *B.C.'s* success in 1967.

In a letter to Michael Carreras, Harryhausen wrote, "The title and its suggested widespread world destruction by another freak flood and earthquake are about all that could be retained of the novel. A much more important new storyline would have to be developed, placing the visual destruction of the world cities in the middle or near the climax of a new concept. A film of this nature has not been on the screen for a long time."
[Walsh, John. *Harryhausen: The Lost Movies*, pp.104]

Ray Harryhausen's concept poster for *Deluge*.

While this may seem only tangentially related to *B.C.,* it goes deeper than that. Ray had some rather unique ideas in terms of how he would update the story. In addition to the ominous eclipse, the moon would leave its orbit, volcanos would erupt, and a "plague of terrifying beasts" would emerge from the ground. Harryhausen confirms in his book, *The Art of Ray Harryhausen*, on page 210 that some of the strange beasts "would be dinosaurs, of course."

Harryhausen was ahead of his time in wanting to do a disaster epic, considering that they would become insanely popular in the 1970s. It's unknown why the 1967 pitch for *Deluge* wasn't accepted by Hammer. Maybe it's because Harryhausen moved onto *Gwangi*.

In *The Art of Ray Harryhausen*, Ray says that he pitched the project to Hammer in 1971. It's unclear if he means to imply this was a second pitch, or if the pitch itself actually occurred in 1971 rather than 1967.

On page 210, he wrote, "I suggested the idea in early 1971 to Michael Carreras, the producer of *One Million Years B.C.* and one of the directors of Hammer Films, but he couldn't see the possibilities."

The last of what could be considered *B.C.'s* unmade spawn is another of Hammer's glamour pictures. [The other unmade prehistoric epics I consider belonging to *When Dinosaurs Ruled the Earth*, which are stories for another time...] The film was to be called *Mistress of the High Seas.* Naturally, Raquel Welch was sought for the title role at various points in the unfinished project's development.

Hammer first flirted with the idea in 1967. It was to be a direct adaptation of John Carlova's novel, *Mistress of the Seas*. It was based on the life of real-life 18th century pirate Anne Bonny. The 1967 version was to be scripted by Carlova himself, and was budgeted at a very large 500,000 pounds!

added the pirate Blackbeard into the mix. Hammer executive Brian Lawrence claimed Guest's script read like a 'girly show'. "I'm not too high on it," he told Michael Carreras in 1974 as the project languished in development.

Oddly, rather than Welch, Hammer wanted Diana Rigg of *On Her Majesty's Secret Service* and TV's *The Avengers* to play the part. MGM wanted someone with more sex appeal, which resulted in the famous Tom Chantrell poster for the prospective film that used Welch's image.

Last Bus to Bray would seem to imply that MGM lost interest in the project, for Hammer also pitched the film to Universal, who rejected it.

And yet, that wasn't the last of Welch as Bonney. In 1978, when Hammer was in its death throes, the project was resurrected again, still with Welch eyed for the part (other sources say Caroline Munro would have played the part now). Rank had agreed to finance the film, which never materialized, likely due to the failure of Hammer's final film, *The Lady Vanishes* in 1979.

For whatever reason, the project sunk and wasn't brought up again until 1973, when MGM expressed interest in distributing it. Hammer began pre-production with a $2.5 million budget in mind. The director of *When Dinosaurs Ruled the Earth*, Val Guest, wrote a screenplay based upon Carlova's earlier script. Guest took a few more liberties with Bonney's life than Carlova did, as he

ENJOYED REMINISCING ABOUT

ONE MILLION B.C. & ONE MILLION YEARS B.C. ?

BUY THE BLU-RAYS, AVAILABLE NOW!

One Million B.C. available from VCI Entertainment.

One Million Years B.C. available from
Kino Lorber Incorporated.

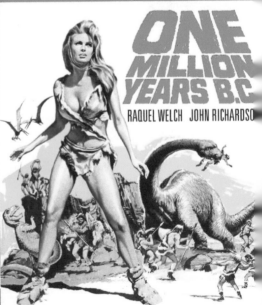

CPSIA information can be obtained
at www.ICGtesting.com
Printed in the USA
LVHW070016110820
662879LV00011B/225